FEMINIZING

HORMONAL

THERAPY

FOR

THE

TRANSGENDERED

means the feminization program is greatly hindered. When we speak of various hormonal regimens, we will give some attention to a particular product called Estraderm - a skin patch and some of the encouraging information that is associated with it in reference to this particular problem will be discussed.

Your physician can acquaint you with some of the signs and symptoms of *phlebitis*, but here is some information to help in your understanding of this condition.

To begin with, there are two vein systems in our bodies - a superficial and a deep one. They interconnect and they function to bring blood that carries carbon dioxide and metabolic waste to our excretory organs and to the heart and lungs for disposal and oxygen replenishment. In a number of situations, they can become inflamed and blood clots can develop. Both are serious and it's when the deep system has clots in it that embolism can take place. The clots can break or detach and go through the vein system to the heart to eventually lodge in the lungs. The degree of clot transport to the lungs determines the severity of the embolic episode. When slight or moderate in the smaller lung veins, the symptoms are chest pain and breathing difficulties. When the blood clots to the lungs are many and large or lodge in major veins to the heart or lungs, then the condition can be catastrophic leading to death. Inflammation in the veins of lower extremities or the pelvic veins of the deep system give pain and often fever along with sudden development of foot, ankle and lower leg swelling. There is immobility and difficulty in walking. Abdomen pain can take place before any chest pains begin. The inflammation and/or clotting of the deep system can be subtle and progressive giving time which allows accurate diagnosis. It can, however, be sudden and overwhelming particularly after trauma or surgery.

Infection in the superficial systems takes place most of the time in the lower extremities, one leg or both. Very seldom does it have embolism associated, although clotting can and does take place. The lower limb becomes painful, swollen and reddened. There may be observed a streak along the course of a superficial vein in the skin. It hurts to walk. Notably complaints may happen overnight or even over several hours.

The diagnosis of phlebitis in either system requires an immediate and often prolonged interruption of the feminizing medical regimen. Treatment will be based on the system involved and the extent of the process in the estimate of the physician by physical examination and laboratory study. Other aspects of underlying health status must be taken into consideration as well.

HYPERTENSION (Elevation of blood pressure)

This can develop in a few patients, or can be accentuated in a few, who already have mild hypertension. In the Free University Hospital of Amsterdam study, the incidence of hypertension overall was just under 5% with two thirds of the group newly diagnosed as having the disorder. All of the 14 patients reported were continued on an estrogen regimen along with appropriate antihypertensive therapy, and they were managed quite successfully. It would seem that it is a concern to be aware of and to be managed appropriately, but not generally a contraindication to hormonal use, unless the degree of pressure elevation is so severe or other complications such as kidney and heart disease develop warranting cessation of the feminizing regimen.

HYPOTHYROIDISM (Under active thyroid disease)

Medical conditions wherein estrogen is used or produced in excess in genetic women, can often times interfere with thyroid activity, often increasing the size of the gland and its workload. This is evident for instance in the first trimester of pregnancy, as with other states of increased estrogen production. On occasion, this is the case for the M-F transgendered person as well. The doctor must be alert to this uncommon but definite endocrine alteration, for it is important to diagnose and to treat. Individuals with thyroid under-activity already in place may need additional thyroid medication once they begin using estrogen, and periodic monitoring of thyroid function is necessary.

PITUITARY CHANGES

You will remember that the pituitary gland produces **prolactin**. Every M-F individual will have an elevation of serum prolactin level once starting estrogen. An occasional one will be elevated quite notably, and if above a specific level that your doctor will know to watch for, some investigation will be proper and alterations may be necessary in your regimen. If the estrogen is stopped and the prolactin levels decrease to acceptable limits, the estrogen can be reinstituted, although in lower doses, for it is known that the increased prolactin levels may be dose-related. If prolactin levels remain in acceptable limits, then the revised regimen can be continued and only periodic serum prolactin determinations need be done. If, however, the levels go back beyond the acceptable limit on the lower doses, or if without estrogen the levels remain higher than acceptable, then the pituitary gland must be evaluated by scanning techniques. This is very important for it implies growth of the gland or perhaps the development of a tumor, known as a prolactinoma within the pituitary gland. One other point to be made is that the anti-androgen, **Androcur**, to be discussed later, will also elevate prolactin levels. This must be considered when a regimen of estrogen and Androcur are used in combination.

This is not a common complication, but it is reported in the medical literature and when such concerning prolactin elevations do occur, your doctor must be certain that other factors are not involved. Stress, exercise programs, alterations in diet and even an underactive thyroid can elevate the serum prolactin. Older age is related as well. Your doctor will be aware of the fact that collection of blood for testing of serum prolactin must be timed, for prolactin production is at its lowest level usually in the later part of the day or in the evening. **Prolactin** production is known to be **pulsatile**, meaning it has peaks and valleys through a 24 hour period.

Changes in vision may also take place with changes in the pituitary. Usually the **serum prolactin levels** in the blood are clues to this before that complaint develops. All hormones must be interrupted and special scanning techniques will be done. Medical treatment with special medicines may be necessary. If that medical therapy does not produce desired results, surgery is the next approach, but this would not be considered without an appropriate consultation with a neurosurgeon.

SEXUAL ACTIVITY

A variety of changes may take place in one's sexual interest and adequacy when taking feminizing hormones. We have already mentioned changes in the penile length and in the size of the testes. These changes alone will influence sexual function. With lower testosterone and lowered or loss of sperm development, infertility can take place. Penile erection is possible but it will not be spontaneous as it was before hormone usage. Stimulation is necessary and the erection in most instances will not be maintained for long. Libido is decreased measurably. The M-F individual for a number of reasons but certainly with estrogen use, may be very passive both in sexual performance and sexual interest or appetite. Penetration may be hampered. Performance may be short lived and of lesser quality. Those who want to preserve male adequacy in sexual relations may experience change that is quite considerable both to their disappointment and the diminished satisfaction of their sexual partner. Orgasm is still possible, but it may have less quality. The whole experience is altered and for the person desiring a regimen for maximal feminization, it should be understood that male sexual activity and satisfaction can be for a great many, altered considerably. Older M-F individuals may note a greater alteration of the sexual experience due to the normal aging process effect on their libido and performance combined with the effects of the hormones.

STONE FORMATION

Gall bladder disease as it occurs more commonly in genetic women much more so during years of estrogen production i.e. fertility years, becomes equally more a reality for the genetic male on estrogen therapy. Some transgendered individuals on hormones feel that their experience with kidney stones has increased on such a regimen as well. There is no reporting in the medical literature to support this later contention however.

CARDIOVASCULAR DISEASE

There is no reason to believe that estrogen has any influence on those forms of heart disease that have to do with the heart valves or with heart rhythm, but there is some concern about coronary vessel disease and the worsening of this process when estrogen is used by genetic males in older age groups. Much of the concern comes from reports in the medical literature of an aggravation of heart disease and increased mortality in men treated with estrogens for prostate cancer. One point must be kept in mind when reading these studies. The male subjects in these studies were in a much older age group with coronary heart disease already in place. Virtually all individuals in these studies were 70 or more years of age.

Information about prior cardiac history in those patients was not given in these studies to any great detail, and in some instances no special prior cardiac study or monitoring was done before the institution of the estrogen regimen. Nor were there any postmortem or autopsy studies accompanying the reporting. The relationship of estrogen use and heart disease in those studies does raise concern but its very difficult to extend information about a study of this sort to a different population, the Transgendered. Generally, the transgendered population using hormones will be notably younger and in better cardiac health. They will be selected for hormone use more carefully than the candidates in a prostatic cancer treatment group. They will be evaluated much more closely before hormones are started. They will be monitored more closely and regularly in their cardiac health while they use hormones. Without doubt, older transgendered individuals desiring hormones must be evaluated much more carefully than younger individuals and then monitored with great care as they continue their programs. But reports in the literature of cardiac death in M-F transgendered individuals using estrogen are relatively uncommon. In a study from the Free University Hospital in Amsterdam of over 700 individuals, 9 developed documented myocardial infarctions (a kind of heart attack), with several having died. In these individuals, a strong family history of coronary heart disease was obtained. Smoking was generally in these patient's daily habits as well. Usually other cardiac health risks can be identified. These include: hypertension, diabetes, obesity and cholesterol imbalances. Patients properly evaluated and observed will generally be identified as possible risks. Monitoring of cardiac status on a regular basis, once the regimen is started, is essential.

The incidence of this serious complication does not seem to be great, although it is very real. Alertness on the part of your physician is mandatory, when dealing with individuals 40 years and older especially. There is every reason to believe however that the same cardio-protective effects of estrogen that benefit the genetic female can be found in the M-F transgendered person on an estrogen regimen.

LIVER FUNCTION

A study of liver activity in the M-F individual is all important in the initial use of an estrogen program, and it must be looked at periodically thereafter. The liver is such a multi-function organ that measurements of certain enzymes and substances in the blood as well as scanning techniques are very necessary for evaluating liver integrity and health. A small percentage of M-F individuals have transient enzyme elevations in these studies with early use of estrogen, but most revert to normal levels in the blood in a short time. Those with persistent abnormalities usually have a prior history of liver insult either from infection or alcohol/drug abuse, or a combination of these. If these disease states are currently active, or if the liver is notably damaged by these entities, then estrogen use can be a further insult and its use must be discontinued, if started at all.

The work of some researchers seems to indicate that a damaged liver does not handle estrogen well and that a healthy liver is generally not troubled by estrogen use and handles it efficiently. Estrogen passes through the liver at different times in its existence in the body and is finally broken down there before it is excreted in changed forms either through the bowel or bladder. Hence, good liver function is important.

EMOTIONAL HEALTH

On a spontaneous basis, transgendered individuals will often disclose what they experience emotionally once they are on hormones. In general, most are quite comfortable and in fact elated. They are finally on a pathway they have wanted to travel for years. They feel wonderful. But some notice a change in their feelings. They have tendency to depression and negativism. How much is attributable to the hormone regimen and how much to current psychosocial alterations in their lives is often hard to evaluate. Nonetheless, there is a distinct number who report such mental changes after beginning treatment, and the greater number of these lose their uncomfortable feelings in a moderate period of time. This implies that outside stresses and pressures in family, work and peer situations, are often more a cause than the medication. In addition, personality variables in the patient may play a very definite role. The likelihood is that very little of this can be attributed **solely** to the hormonal regimen. Still suicide or attempts to commit suicide are of concern to professionals in their reports to the medical literature. I find it hard to blame medication alone for such emotional instability and self-destructive attempts. I think the transgendered, especially the trans-sexual, has so much to cope with in life, trying to find congruence, acceptance and stability, that the mental climate for some is extremely troubled.

MISCELLANEOUS COMPLAINTS

A number of lesser concerns may be evident as the hormonal regimen continues. Individuals sometimes experience a number of gastrointestinal disorders such as nausea or abdominal pain. Digestive and elimination problems may develop with estrogen, especially when using oral preparations. Skin rash, localized or generalized, nail brittleness and fluid retention, are all occasional complaints. Infrequently, an individual may have problems with glasses requiring periodic examinations or may show inability to wear contact lens because of changes in the front-to-back diameter of the globe of the eye. Headaches take place with hormone use in both genetic females and genetic males. If very difficult and unrelenting, the hormones should be stopped for a time to determine a relationship between this complaint and the medication. Keep in mind, however, headaches can have multiple causes, such as sinus disease, dental and eye disorders, stress and neck vertebrae arthritis to name only a few. Consider other causes always and get a check up if they persist. These annoyances, if estrogen-related, rarely cause such a problem that the estrogen must be discontinued. Institution of a different regimen—a different product, dosage or route of administration—can be helpful.

Chapter 6 Overview
- Annoyances, although not life-threatening, often occur with a contragender regimen
- Serious problems and complications can occur on a contragender regimen
- Periodic evaluation by a competent physician is vital to avoid and possibly correct potential problems or serious concerns while on a feminizing regimen
- Be certain that your physician possesses adequate medical knowledge in contragender hormonal care and treatment.
- If your physician lacks adequate knowledge in treatment and management--get another physician!

Chapter 7   Problems and Annoyances
You Might Experience on Progesterone

By and large progesterone is limited in its effects on the genetic male. It does not have the influence in stimulating feminization or influencing bodily tissues as extensively as does estrogen. Its real value in the M-F individual is in its stimulus to breast development. In subprimate studies, progesterone does affect breast gland tissue development, and in older medical literature, it was thought that progesterone had a very important role in the female breast for its development in puberty and maintenance through the reproductive years. Recent literature does not fully confirm this, but it is reasonable to believe that progesterone given in a cyclic manner, as it is in some regimens, is responsible along with estrogen in promoting breast growth in the genetic male. It was this view that prompted the Benjamin regimen of hormonal use back in the 1930's and as it is given by some physicians even now.

Progesterone can be considered a mild testosterone antagonist, a suppressant or an anti-androgen of a sort. As such when given with an estrogen in a cyclic manner as in older regimens it can help to potentate the estrogen but more effective anti-androgens are now available. It may not be as important in today's treatment plan as once thought.

However, progesterone has no strong influence on the skin, hair, nails, or on fat deposition, and no effect upon voice and limited effect upon the male genitalia, though certainly not to the extent estrogen does. It will, as can estrogen, cause some discomforts and complications. It can be responsible for fluid retention and edema, for personality and mood shifts, for phlebitis, and for changes, as noted with estrogen, in the eye globe diameter. Also as with estrogen, it can cause skin rashes, nausea and vomiting, headache and libido change and even at times for some, severe acne.

Progesterone can also influence certain systems in your biochemistry. Its influence is not noted in the pituitary with prolactin elevation or generally in the liver with various enzyme changes. Principal changes in our body chemistry because of progestational use have to do with lipid metabolism. Progesterone does everything in a manner relatively opposite to estrogen. In contrast, progesterone raises serum cholesterol and the LDL fraction. It also lowers the HDL fraction. This change in the serum lipid profile can promote adverse blood vessel change and therefore a tendency to develop heart disease. Progesterone and some other specific progestational products tend to be "androgenic". As we have noted, androgenicity leads to adverse arterial change and to risk for heart disease. There may be a canceling out of the good effects of estrogen when estrogen and progesterone products are used together. If progesterone has such tendency to influence a particular individual in this way, prolonged use puts that individual at risk for poor health. This could be an argument against its use in an estrogen hormonal regimen. I believe that progesterone products have value in regimens for some genetic males in a selective manner, but not for all. Some physicians will not give it to their patients and state this in the medical literature.

Chapter 7 Overview

- Progesterone can be used in feminization although it's not as effective as other medications.

- Use of progesterone can add to the potential for complications i.e. phlebitis or fluid retention

- Individuals with cholesterol elevation or altered HDL/Cholesterol ratio may not be candidates for Progesterone use

Chapter 8   *Medications Available and Regimens In Current Use*

There is no uniformity as yet in the medical literature as to the kind of medications or the dosage to be used for the M-F individual desiring feminization. In theory, the best regimen I believe is an estrogen in moderate dosage in combination with an anti-androgen. To give example - an initial or starting dose of **Premarin** or **Estinyl** lower than usual for maintenance would be quite appropriate for 2 or 3 months. It is wise to use the estrogen alone for a time before introducing the anti-androgen. With all acceptable in the physician's and patient's evaluation of its initial use, then the anti-androgen can be introduced, again in dosage lower than maintenance. With appropriate time passage and acceptance of the combination by both the physician and the patient once again both medications can be increased to maintenance levels and periodic monitoring begins. All physical, biochemical and subjective changes have to be in order as the regimen is moved to appropriate dosages.

The guidelines your physician will consider will be your sense of good health and well being, and your gradual, but definite, physical alteration along with stability in your laboratory studies. He or she should evaluate your liver enzymes, your lipid profiles, thyroid studies, prolactin levels, and look for decrease in your serum testosterone to genetic female levels-all as we discussed in a previous chapter.

Is there room for other regimens? Yes, there is, and

there are a number of them reported in the medical literature. Some physicians use injectable estrogen to supplement the oral estrogen regimen. Some use oral medication alone. Others will use an injectable long-acting anti-androgen which lasts approximately a month. Some doctors prefer only an oral anti-androgen. What is most important is that your physician be knowledgeable and adaptable enough to change regimen and dosages as necessary. When laboratory values, subjective feelings and physical changes or complaints arise that are adverse, the regimen needs to be modified to fit the circumstances. He or she must be prepared to do this and to bring everything back to a level of comfort and acceptance for both the patient and the physician. Some transgendered individuals may have expectations that won't ever be accomplished. Sometimes more can be accomplished in physical change with reasonable alterations in the regimen. Both you and your physician should be in good agreement and in good cooperative attitude to accomplish the best in the safest way.

I do not endorse any specific hormonal regimen, but I do emphasize the need for moderation, for careful monitoring, and for patience. This formula works over time.

Several Points To Keep In Mind:

1. Dosage need not be more than moderate. Excessive doses of a product are to no avail and in fact, invite complications. The medical literature supports this view.

2. Tissue response and time will bring to you virtually all that you are capable of accomplishing. There is no shortcut to alteration of physical characteristics. Hereditary tendency and tissue response to a hor-

mone are to be kept in mind and time is required to accomplish results.

3. Routes of administration will depend upon physician preference and past experience. There is available a topical approach for the M-F person. Oral preparations work just as well as *intramuscular* (injections) preparations in the M-F. The injection approach may be more expedient for some. Oral medications may take a bit more time, but that can be very much an advantage in avoiding complications. Needles are a difficult regimen for anyone to experience and mean an increase in office visits and costs unless you self inject.

4. *17 Beta Estradiol* is a much more potent estrogen than those constituents, for instance, in Premarin, and those products containing it may be more preferred by physicians in their programs. This is something to discuss with your physician.

5. Try not to make a comparison between yourself and others in various degrees of progress particularly in breast development. You both may be on the very same regimen, yet you may feel that they are moving along much more efficiently. Don't fall into this trap. Keep in mind, that we all react to medication differently. You may not have the same level of tissue reactivity as some one else. This isn't to say that discussion with your physician is not in order. For some medication changes may accomplish more for one person than for the another. Keep in mind, however, that not all individuals reach the same level of success in all ways.

ESTROGENS

Oral Preparations

As mentioned, *17 Beta Estradiol* is the most potent estrogen to be offered. It is the principal agent in some of the following:

Estinyl

This particular medicine contains ethinyl estradiol and comes in doses that range from 0.02 mg. to 0.05 mg. Use of the 0.05 mg. dose once each day would be quite adequate for most individuals and less should be ordered if the individual becomes postoperative. A few individuals could use two 0.05 mg. tablets daily, but clinical response, testosterone levels, and absence of changes in health, will be the guide for this and any other dosage.

Estrace

This medication contains *17 Beta Estradiol* and comes in 1.0 mg. and 2.0 mg. tablets. Usually, a 2.0 mg. per day tablet is an adequate dose with which to maintain. Increments will again depend upon physical change, testosterone levels, and absence of side effects or impairments to health.

Premarin

This is a very familiar estrogen preparation which contains a number of different estrogens along with *17 Alpha Estradiol*. It is obtainable in doses of 0.3 mg. to 2.5 mg. with quite a few doses in between. Initial trials with 1.25 mg. daily would be appropriate, and with satisfaction on your part and that of your physician, there is allowance for increasing that dosage gradually, up to as much as 5.0 mg. per day. Doses above this are in excess, and there is creditable work reported in the medical literature to substantiate this. Again, time and tissue response is the key, not high doses.

Estrovis

This is a synthetic analog of **ethinyl estradiol** which comes in 100 mcg. tablets. Starting with 100 mcg. daily to be sure that the medication is tolerable is appropriate, and then an increase as is indicated would be in order.

Ogen

This is an analog of **estrone** which contains a very active estrogenic substance. It comes in a number of doses and likely no more than the number 5 Ogen would be necessary on a daily basis as a maintenance dose. Once again, initial dose and subsequent maintenance medication would depend on clinical response, serum testosterone suppression, and the absence of any undesired effects.

Injectable Preparations

Injectable medications are available and offered by many physicians. The real value of this approach is this:

- Theoretically, the liver is involved in processing the estrogen only once.

- More continuous and constant estrogenic effect is obtained by this depository route of administration.

Often physicians use this approach to hasten physical change in order to satisfy the impatience of their transgendered patient. It can help in this regard, but to rush this process in my view is not wise, no matter what the request or apparent need. The products available for this approach are the following:

Estradurin

This product contains *17 Beta Estradiol* and is offered in a 20 mg. to 40 mg. dosage by injection every two to four weeks.

Delestrogen

This product is available in both aqueous and oil preparations available for short-acting or long-acting use. Generally, long-acting is preferred, and a dose of 20-40 mg. every two to four weeks is ideal.

Estrogen Valerate

A very worthwhile injectable estrogen. 20 mg injected every two weeks is the normal dosage.

Topical Preparations

Estrogen creams are available. **Premarin, Ogen,** and **Estrace** creams are examples. Some individuals will use these per rectum to accomplish mild physical change. I don't recommend this approach, nor do I think there is much value in using these products on the skin over various body surfaces. However, some who apply a cream directly to the breasts will experience a mild change in size and sensitivity. Some individuals feel that application of an estrogen cream to the balding areas of the scalp is beneficial. These experiences generally are observed only by a few.

One topical approach which is of great worth it would seem from reports in the medical literature is an estrogen patch called **Estraderm**. Genetic women have used this product for several years. Its usual use is in replacing estrogen in those who are post-menopausal. The patch comes in two dosages--0.05 and 0.1 and *17 Beta Estradiol* is the estrogen delivered to the body through the skin. There is an on-going study in the European medical literature wherein both pre- and postoperative M-F transsexuals have been using 100 mcg. (0.1) of 17 Beta Estradiol in an estrogen patch with very favorable results in accomplishing feminization and maintaining it. The patch is changed every second or third day, rotated to different areas of the torso, and the only drawbacks seem to be the fact that local skin irritation sometimes is quite notable in some, and that this mode of therapy can be considerably more expensive than oral medication.

Keep in mind the following in the use of the Estraderm Patch:

1. The Estroderm patch should be considered in the hormonal regimens of all M-F individuals above the age of 40, either pre- or postoperative according to the Amsterdam study. It accomplishes very adequate physical change in combination with an anti-androgen.

2. According to the Amsterdam study, it can be used in M-F individuals whose regimen of estrogen use has been interrupted because of the complication of phlebitis and/or embolism (blood clot to the lungs). A series of postphlebitic individuals have been studied and followed with use of the topical *Estraderm* patch, and none have had recurrent vein or blood clot problems. Heretofore, this group would never be permitted estrogen again. With the skin patch, their regimen can be reinstituted.

In my view, estrogen therapy can be a continuous one. There is likely no need to interrupt, or use the medication on a cyclic basis, as it was at one time offered to the transgendered population by physicians who followed the Harry Benjamin technique.

PROGESTERONE

Oral Preparations

The products that are commonly in use are these:

Provera

Known as **medroxyprogesterone**, it is available in a 2.5 mg., 5.0 mg and 10 mg. tablet. Usually, 10 mg. is used in the last ten days of each month, and I prefer this approach when it is used, but some physicians will give this on a daily basis along with estrogen, never interrupting the two.

Aygestin

Known as **norethindrone acetate**, this comes in a 5 mg. tablet. Either 5 or 10 mg. could be used in the last ten days of each month. Once again, I prefer only cyclic use of progesterone when it is to be considered in a regimen. Some physicians prefer continuous use.

Other products are available. **Cycrin, Norlutate** and **Norlutin** are oral progesterones that your doctor may choose in place of others. They are equally as effective as the other preparations that I have mentioned.

Injectable Preparations

There is one injectable progesterone very commonly used, known as **Depoprovera**. This is an aqueous suspension of progesterone and it can be given in 100 or 200 mg. doses once per month.

ANTI-ANDROGENS

A very important class of medications to be considered in the feminization process are the **anti-androgens**. This group is of particular importance and value in that they suppress testosterone not only from the testes, but also from the adrenal gland. This is a very diverse group of drugs. While they have use in treating other disorders, their one common effect for the M-F individual is the **reduction of testosterone activity**. This may take place either by inhibiting testosterone production or by limiting conversion of testosterone once produced to a more active form, **Dihydrotestosterone**---or by interfering with testosterone incorporation into the cells of various tissues (organs) that depend upon its influence.

When given in combination with an appropriate estrogen, these medications can be very effective in the feminization process. The M-F person has the advantage when using this class of drugs, of using lower doses of estrogen, and minimizing the potential for estrogen side effects.

The first of these medications to consider is a product used widely in the United States called **Spironolactone** or **Aldactone.** It is a potent diuretic and anti-hypertensive. Taken by mouth, it is given in doses of 100-300 mg. a day at peak maintenance, although in the regimen used by physicians at the Vancouver Hospital in British Columbia, Canada, considerably larger daily doses have been used. Its ordinary use to counter mild to moderate hypertension makes it an ideal in selected hypertensive transgendered patients as well, for they can have therapy for blood pressure elevation as well as the feminization program. Electrolytes must be evaluated periodically since this is a special kind of diuretic which saves potassium rather than depletes it in the stores of this electrolyte in our system. Your doctor will understand its use and the monitoring that is necessary when you use it.

The next most frequently used anti-androgen is an injectable product called **Lupron** (acetate of leuprolide). Formerly it was given as a subcutaneous injection on a daily basis. Now as a depository medication, **Lupron** is given once every four weeks by injection utilizing a 3.75 mg. dose. It works very effectively to suppress testosterone. There are however, two major drawbacks to this medication. The first is expense, and the second is that some individuals experience a moderate amount of musculoskeletal discomfort and have potential for cardiovascular difficulties. Fluid retention, blood pressure changes, and symptoms attributable to decreased blood flow to the heart, are known with this medication. Unfortunately, there is not enough reporting for this medication in the transgendered medical literature, even though a sizable population is using it.

There are other products that have value for a feminization regimen and are in use although no notable studies have been reported to the medical community. These are:

Eulexin (flutamide)

This medication is used ordinarily to treat metastatic prostatic cancer.

Finasterid (Proscar)

This medicine is used generally to treat urinary complaints due to benign prostatic hypertrophy or enlargement.

Nizoral (ketoconazole)

This a broad spectrum anti-fungal agent. This medication works very well to inhibit testosterone production and is used in a 200-400 mg. daily dose. There is a warning however, with this medication. It is injurious to the liver for some individuals and transgendered patients who have a history of liver disease in the past must be monitored very carefully, if they are candidates for it at all. There are some reports also that *Nizoral* is not effective over a long period of time, and that eventually some individuals building a tolerance to it, do not accomplish as much testosterone suppression as when first using it.

I want to acquaint you with a medication not as yet available in the United States though obtainable in Canada, Mexico and in Europe. There is a moderate amount of experience and reporting that exists with use of this anti-androgen, and its use in the transgendered population as an accompaniment to estrogen is quite well established in Europe.

Androcur (cyproterone acetate)

This was first used in Germany as a drug to curb deviant sexual behavior in non-transgendered males. It can be used because of its notable suppressive activity on testosterone production in the M-F individual. It is generally given in 100 mg. doses daily and used with great success, although there are a few considerations that must be kept in mind.

Firstly, for some, liver toxicity is a concern and it can alter blood sugar levels as well. The latter would be of concern in the diabetic transgendered person. Occasional individuals also note irritability, mood swings, and fatigue, and in spite of the very effective feminizing effects, those complaints could be severe enough to warrant interruption. As mentioned, *Androcur* can also have an effect upon prolactin and could be a notable concern with excessive levels.

Once again it is important to emphasize-the combination of an anti-androgen with an estrogen preparation— both in appropriate dosage is a very ideal regimen for the feminization process.

Birth Control Pills

Many will be motivated to use birth control pills usually prescribed for someone else. Occasionally doctors order them as a feminizing regimen. In the past, these contraceptive pills contained large doses of both **estrogen** and **progesterone**. Because of the increased incidence of stroke and serious heart attacks in women using them, investigation conducted by pharmaceutical companies revealed that the dosages of progesterone and the incorporation of certain progestational products in the pills were responsible for the increase in stroke and heart attacks.

Blood lipids were discovered to be notably affected, leading to serious artery changes (arterioclerosis). A definite change in the manufacturing of the birth control pill took place. Dosages were lowered and synthetic progesterone products with decidedly little "testosterone like" changes to the blood lipid components were developed. Currently the pills in use contain principally progesterone and very little estrogen. It's not a proper regimen for feminization and if used without physician monitoring--it is potentially dangerous. Can there be some feminization? Yes, but the process in not ideal and not recommended.

Natural Occurring Hormones

Many natural occurring substances, foods, herbs, and

other plants-time honored and fully recognized as having hormone influence in our bodies are available in drug stores and health food stores. Some are processed into powders, pills and additives of various kinds. Some are sold in original form. And they do work to some extent although minimal feminization will take place. Many individuals report that with using them they do experience some physical alterations. But there are several things to keep in mind in using these products. To begin with there is very little way to know how much active hormone is taken at any time. There is often no accurate standardization as there is when using hormones made by a pharmaceutical company. Consequently response will be variable and often times minimal. In addition, these products in delivering hormonal effect to various physiological systems in our body still need to be monitored-and most individuals using them don't realize that. They don't understand that they should be under a physician's care in the much the same way as for prescribed medication. While it is true this approach is less expensive and for those not in a doctor's care there are no medical fees or laboratory charges to pay, the pathway to successful feminization is inefficient, unrewarding, and could be for some a real health concern. This approach is really homeopathic medicine and just as it is not advisable to use excessive medication, it is not really an advantage to use a program such as this.

Summary

The guidelines for your physician will always be your well being and gradual but continuing physical change as demonstrated in your periodic examinations. Breast measurements, hip and waist ratios, and diminution in penile length and testes size are all important to assess with each visit. Laboratory evaluations will be very important, and they must include liver and lipid profiles, serum prolactin, and a serum testosterone level. The testosterone test helps greatly in assessing the biochemical status of the male to female individual. An end point in that assessment is to attain blood levels of this male hormone, as found in the genetic female.

Once again, I caution you in that you should not use more than prescribed each day no matter what regimen you are placed on. For example, researchers agree that dosages above 5 mg. of **Premarin** each day invite medical complication. All that is possible for you in specific to accomplish, will take place with non-excessive dosage over time. Dosage should be graduated to the maintenance level. As an example, if we were to begin with 1.25 mg. of **Premarin** taken daily, and there was good tolerance for this dosage, in perhaps two months it could be increased to 2.5 mg. Adding an ***anti-androgen*** at that point to the increased dosage of ***estrogen*** would be appropriate. After a period of observation, both medications could be increased, keeping in mind that physical well being, changes in physical status and blood testosterone determinations along with other lab data would be guidelines to taking dosage to safe maximum.

Injectable ***estrogens*** may hasten the process. An added concern in their use is that they may put you in some measure of risk, when they are combined with oral ***estrogen***. There could be higher estrogen levels in your system than is appropriate. To try and accomplish too much in too short a period of time invites complication.

Progestational products can be used in combination with estrogen and even with an anti-androgen as several researchers report in the medical literature. My concern with medications such as **Provera** or **Aygestin** is that while they affect favorably breast tissue, they add to the risk of phlebitis and to the annoyance of fluid retention. Also, they can act to reverse the benefits of estrogen on your lipid profile. In addition, some researchers say frankly that it is not necessary to use it.

Looking once again at the role of the **anti-androgen** in the hormonal regimen, we are reminded of a very important consideration. These medications work very effectively to lower the testosterone pool in the blood, not only that contributed by the testes, but also testosterone coming from the adrenal gland as well. This is very important in the therapy and can allow for lower estrogen doses which lessen the chance of complication. This is why I champion this regimen. The hope is that in the very near future the Federal Drug Administration will allow use of Androcur in the United States, for it is most effective in the hormonal regimens of M-F individuals elsewhere.

One additional thought—regimens wherein there are days with no medication taken as in a cyclic approach seem to be unnecessary. It was once thought to be a proper approach in the past but not important to do so currently.

Chapter 8 Overview

- **NEVER exceed recommended dosages. To do so greatly risks your health.**

- Patience and time are important ingredients during the contragender regimen

- Individuals respond differently to hormonal treatment. This variance is based on your own biological make up—not necessarily the contragender regimen

- Regimens and dosages can be modified to accomplish the optimal results on the advice of your physician. Safety should not be sacrificed and should always be kept in mind

- **Discuss the possibility of Anti-androgens with your physician. They are often underprescribed because their real value is often unrecognized.**

Chapter 9   *Periodic Monitoring On A Feminization Regimen*

One of the very important considerations for both you and your physician to keep in mind once a hormone regimen has begun is the need for ongoing monitoring. The fact the regimen may change in product and dosage, that you may have one or several intolerances to the hormones that you use, that you may not make progress in the body changes that you are capable of - all these and more should impress you with the knowledge that the first year or so of contragendered hormonal treatment demands periodic reassessment and re-evaluation.

Once a hormonal regimen is initiated the changes in the medications are directly related to the physical examination, changes in the laboratory results and careful consideration of how you feel with this new hormonal influence. Your physician will want to know how you feel and to what extent and should not be satisfied with only physical change. Your physician should make inquiry into your emotions and what you are experiencing in your social interchange with others in your life--whether it be family, acquaintances or the workplace.

Your monitoring physical examination will be much shorter an evaluation than the initial one but it must include your weight, blood pressure (both arms), your heart and lungs and an inspection of your lower extremities for fluid retention and changes, if any, in the veins. Laboratory studies will include your lipid profile, liver profile, a blood prolactin and testosterone level. If any blood tests in the last examination warrant restudy this should be included. Special studies may be added relative to past lab reports or complaints you may voice at this time. As subsequent visits take place some testing may be less necessary and the frequency of visits will lessen. To give example; if there have been elevations of certain enzymes with no known history of liver disease or injury to this organ those transient elevations can be expected to revert to normal in a short while. If not, the liver must be evaluated and hormones may need to be interrupted. With continued comfort in your use of the medications and normal results in all your examinations, your regimen can be enhanced. Measurements of breasts, hips, waist and derriere should be made periodically by you or your doctor and compared with previous information. If you are smoking, your progress with cutting down or cutting out should be a part of the discussion. Instructions relative to diet and weight control are very much a part of each visit. As you progress to a year of hormone use, your visits could take place every six months depending on progress or complication. With visits stretched out to a year apart, the same evaluations that took place in your very first visit before the institution of hormones will need to be repeated-that is a thorough physical, all appropriate laboratory work, an interval EKG and special studies as indicated. Your doctor and your mental health care professional either a psychologist, social worker or psychiatrist should exchange information about you periodically. That exchange can be helpful in their management of you and will be invaluable to your progress. If for any reason you must leave the care of a professional, your records should be available to the next one who assumes your care. Record keeping is very important and those records are yours to direct to another doctor or mental health care professional.

Chapter 9 Overview

- **Once again, periodic monitoring CANNOT be stressed enough**

- **Acquaint yourself with the recommended monitoring process and inform your physician that you want it to be followed**

- **Arrange for your medical records to be transferred and shared with any medical or health care professional by whom you are cared for. Information exchanged between all your care providers means better care for you**

Chapter 10 *Measurements - A Way to Evaluate Progress*

To take measurements of the waist, the hips, the derriere and the breasts can be very encouraging to you. To appreciate progress, even a small amount consistently each time the measurements are recorded is very important. Once a month, and probably no more often is what I recommend. Bring the measurements to your physician each visit. They should be placed in his or her records as well. While I believe your doctor should take them, in most instances, he or she will most likely depend on you. Your measurements should be taken in the same manner, each and every time, to have relevance, so certain landmarks are necessary to become familiar with. It is important as well to use a soft cloth measuring tape as that which is used by a tailor or a dressmaker. Stand before a mirror, preferably one which gives you complete view of your whole body or certainly from the pubic hair line to the top of your head.

Breast Measurements

Look at your breasts. You want to establish landmarks that make your periodic measurements consistent. Look at the nipple on the left breast. Elevate your gaze to a point on the collar bone directly above the nipple. Place the end of the tape on that point on the collar bone and let the tape drop down over the breast. You are holding the tape with fingers of your **left** hand. With the **right** hand gently guide the tape directly over the nipple and tuck the flexible tape into the crevice beneath the breast. (This crevice is the space below the inframammary ridge.) The tape should be against but not compressing the nipple. Fix that point in the crevice on the tape with finger and thumb of the right hand. (Refer to Figure 3, Line AB.) Take the tape away from the chest wall and read it in inches. Then record the measurement in a log that you keep for this purpose.

Once again standing before the mirror, look at the **armpit** (axilla) to the **left** of your left breast. Place the end of the tape with your **right** hand just inside the fold of the **left** arm and **left** chest wall. This is the **Anterior Axillary Line**. Hold it in that place with fingers of the **left** hand and extend the tape down to a point of the left chest wall directly in line with the **left** breast nipple. (Refer to Figure 3, Line CD.) Take the tape out of the axilla and place the end of it at that point, extending it across the **left** breast over the nipple without compression, to the center of the breast bone between the breasts. Grasp the tape with the thumb and finger of the **right** hand, remove it from the chest wall, read the measurement in inches and record it. (Line DE)

You now have two measurements of the **left** breast. As time passes with continued hormone use these measurements should increase depending upon your individual tissue response. You should recognize changes in size and volume in these two measurements. The first measurement is a **vertical** one - the second is a **lateral** measurement.

Let's examine this measurement technique a bit more. You may ask- how can I be certain my measurement landmarks will be consistently the same? One way to insure that is to mark the reference points on the **col-**

lar bone and at ***Anterior Axillary Line*** across from the nipple and on the *left* chest with washable ink. Position the tape measure at these ink marks. The center of the chest could be marked but it is not altogether necessary. Another question you might ask is that in previous publications, I asked for hemi-circumferencial measurements in cms. Why have I changed the method of measurement? I find of late that doctors don't take these measurements and that the responsibility lies with you. I think that this new technique is easier for you, more meaningful and more accurate. You may wonder if it is necessary to measure both breasts. The answer is "yes." The breasts can develop in an asymmetric way, one breast growing more than the other or even with a slightly different shape. Genetic women experience this. It really means little. The important thing is the gradual increase in each over time. The same technique outlined above can be applied to the measurement of the right breast.

Lastly, after about two years on an adequate feminizing regimen the breast will be at maximal growth or very near to it. At this time, measurements can be stopped.

Waist Measurement

To measure the **waist** is easy to do unless weight gain is an appreciable problem. This measurement with no weight increase or loss of abdominal muscle tone should consistently stay the same. Place the tape around the body in the space just below the ribs. (Refer to Figures 1 and 2, Line #1.) Don't inhale. Take the measurement in inches and record it. (Watch your calories, continue to exercise and don't gain weight.)

Hip Measurement

To measure the **hips**, search for a bony prominence on either side just below your waistline measurement. These two areas are the very top of the bones that form the pelvic complex. It is a convenient and non-moving landmark. Place the tape measure directly over these bony prominences on both sides as you place the tape around your body. (Refer to line #2 in figures 1 and 2.) Read the tape and record in inches.

Derriere Measurement

To measure the **derriere**, place the tape around the buttocks at what you will estimate is the midpoint of the "cheeks." Bring one end of the tape to a point at the top of the pubic hairline and extend the other "leg" of the tape across it. (Refer to line #3 in figures 1 and 2.) Take a measurement where they meet and record it. Overtime it will gradually change indicating increased fat deposition in this area.

Chapter 10 Overview

- **Measure yourself in the same manner each time and no more than once a month.**

- **Measurement calculations will most probably be your task. Share them with your physician for inclusion in your records**

- **For accurate measurements, use the diagrams and methods included in this chapter**

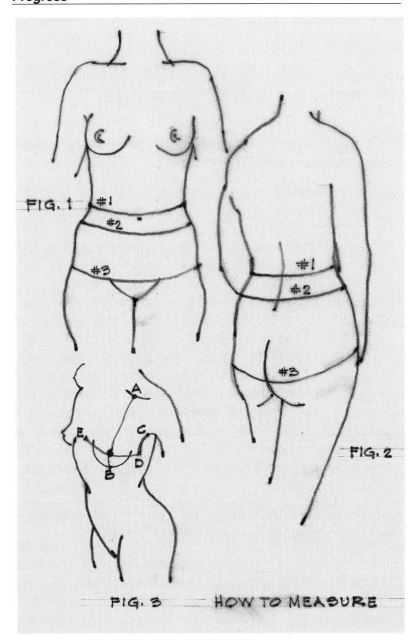

FIG. 1

FIG. 2

FIG. 3   HOW TO MEASURE

Chapter 11   Questions Commonly Asked

Do I have a worry in regard to developing breast cancer with my use of estrogen?

The medical literature contains only four reported cases of breast cancer in male individuals using a feminizing regimen over the past twenty or more years. This is very encouraging. It would appear that the incidence of this malignancy is no greater than noted in the male population not using estrogen and that probably the incidence is quite low. Does it mean that with the high doses that M-F Transgendered use over long periods of time that there is still no risk? That remains to be seen. Does it mean that family history for breast cancer in M-F individuals using estrogen can be ignored? That also is a question that needs to be answered. A study to look at these and other possibilities has to be done. In the meantime, self-breast examination and periodic mammography are very important things to do until more is known about this concern.

Should my chromosomes be counted to determine why I am transgendered?

The number of transgendered males with abnormal chromosome counts are small. Most transgendered individuals will have normal counts. The question to answer is should all transgendered persons have a chromosome profile done as a routine. It is expensive and the numbers of abnormalities found will be so small as to consider this testing only if suspicion exists in the mind of the doctor or patient.

Can I take hormones even if I do not intend to have genital reassignment surgery?

Yes. There is reason to prescribe hormones for male transgendered who want to feminize with no plan to have genital reassignment surgery. The number of "non-operative" transsexuals and other transgendered on the spectrum who want hormones even intermittently but will never consider reassignment seems to be increasing. The procedures for placing these transgendered on a feminizing program are the same. They should be evaluated by a mental health care professional and they must be in the care of medical physician who understands the evaluation process and therapy. They must also know the possibilities and the consequences of such a major step. If individuals change their minds some changes may be permanent.

Why must I stop smoking when I use estrogen as a part of my feminizing process?

There are hundreds of substances in tobacco. One in large quantity is nicotine. This drug acts to alter arteries and the heart in their functions. Tobacco use adds to the hardening of the arteries process as well, because of its effect on the blood lipids. These changes can be very hazardous. So much has been reported in the medical and lay literature about the hazards of smoking. When estrogen can satisfy such a real need in the transgendered person, why smoke to undo it?

I want to have a baby. Will hormone use help me to achieve this desire?

Definitely not. The male using hormones has none of the essential internal genitalia (uterus and ovaries) for conceiving a baby or bringing it to maturation or even viability. Even in-vitro fertilization techniques as used in genetic women who have fertility problems require a uterus to receive the implanted pregnancy. In a male, a fertilized egg would have to be implanted in the abdomen. Even if it would attach and grow, the dangers of causing bleeding and other serious if not fatal complications within the abdomen would be great. The pregnancy would not find enough nutrition because of limited placental growth. The pregnancy would not progress for very long. The event of abdominal pregnancy even in genetic women is EXTREMELY rare and associated with great risk and a high rate of pregnancy failure.

Can I breast feed a baby once I take hormones?

Once the breast begins the growth process, it is possible to put an infant to breast and to suckle. In most instances, however, the male breast will produce no milk spontaneously. Another medication is needed to produce milk. If milk production begins, you must realize this milk will likely have poor nutritional value in comparison with milk from the genetic female breast. The milk will be scant in volume and will not be constant in production. The male breast could stop producing if the chemical stimuli for milk production is not constant. And that stimuli is not an easy thing to accomplish. The genetic male just doesn't have all the physiology development and nerve pathways that the genetic female possesses to breast feed. There is another consideration to keep in mind - the male who produces milk could have pituitary growth or tumor that is responsible for the production of milk.

Can I expect my sex drive and my sexual performance to be the same once I start taking feminizing hormones?

No! Your interest in sex will change considerably. You will not be interested in sexual relations as much, if at all, once hormone use is at peak. When you do have relations, spontaneous erection will not be possible except upon self-stimulus or by your partner. Penetration will be difficult if not impossible. Sustaining erection will not be easy and the ejaculate will diminish or disappear. However, even though intercourse may be difficult or impossible, many report that their ability to reach intense excitement and satisfaction with their partners through other methods of sexual stimulation is quite possible.

Will I ever menstruate?

No. It's not possible. You don't have a uterus to respond to your hormone therapy. Even if you elect to have genital reassignment surgery a uterus will not be placed in your body.

Can I obtain an ovary transplant?

In China, a small series of Male to Female Transsexuals were operated on in this way and in preliminary study they did produce estrogen and did have some feminization. Most of them had failure of the transplanted ovary. The few remaining have not been reported on in recent medical literature.

So to answer your question, yes, it is possible to have ovary transplantation. However, I know of no physician except the one in China who has experimented with this procedure and the results of this experimentation is far from optimal.

Why do I have to continue my hormones after genital reassignment surgery?

Without estrogen after your surgery, you will experience osteoporosis (brittle bone disease). Spontaneous fractures will occur and your health will be notably impaired because the sex hormones are necessary to many organ systems.

After surgery, your dosage will be lowered. But if discontinued altogether, your quality of life will be greatly altered and typical menopausal complaints along with osteoporosis will plague you.

Is it necessary to have all the testing suggested? Not all doctors order these tests so why are they important?

Doctors who don't monitor your health in the correct ways with examinations and laboratory studies are playing with your health. These tests are important to gather information about your health and to monitor any possible changes that could effect your well being. If you don't insist on proper evaluations, you also are jeopardizing your health.

How long will it take to have the full effects of hormones take place in my body?

The optimal results on an adequate and properly maintained feminizing regimen should be seen within two years. The process should not be accelerated by increasing medications or tampering with dosages. This can be dangerous and even fatal. It takes time to reverse testosterone effects and to change tissues with estrogenic influences. If expectations are too high or fanciful and there is impatience in the treatment process, one flirts with potentially serious complications.

Can I stop and start hormones at will? And if I do so, after breast development, can I keep my ability to have an erection?

Some people play at this. It's probable that some things can be accomplished or kept in place with this method but maximal feminine change won't be accomplished as effectively as with a constant hormonal plan. You invite complications as well by intermittent or interrupted use - particularly phlebitis. The idea of having the best of both worlds is not a good or effective one.

If I develop fairly good breast development and then stop hormones will the breast changes go away?

No. The development will stay but maintenance of good breast tissue will lessen. The texture, firmness and suppleness will diminish. In many ways they will become such as seen in the genetic woman's menopausal breast.

---

*REMEMBER--*NO* question asked is foolish or irrelevant.

Write to me with yours or for additional information at this address:

Sheila Kirk, M.D.
P.O. 38114
Blawnox, PA 15238-9998
Telephone: (412) 781-1092   Fax (412) 781-1096

Chapter 12   Self-Breast Examinations

The incidence of serious breast disease—malignancy for the genetic male on a hormonal regimen, appears to be no greater than for the genetic male not using a hormonal regimen. But benign breast changes can take place. Thickening, cysts and strange collections or buildup of tissue can develop and it is important to detect them and bring attention of these to your physician for accurate evaluation. Hence, I strongly urge you to learn the technique of self-breast examination described below and to conduct it once, every month, on a specific date or day.

Admittedly, if you have had breast augmentation with a saline, or a silicone prosthesis, the examination is more difficult. Yet in time, your awareness as to what is the usual in your own breasts becomes very accurate. The technique is not difficult. There are no shortcuts and thoroughness is important.

The technique is as follows --Lying down in supine position (on your back,) you will examine the left breast with the right hand, the right breast with the left hand. If you are full-breasted, it helps a little to place a pillow at your back with its inner margin just up to and in the length of the spine, thereby tipping you somewhat. Hence, the pillow is to the right side of your back and spine to examine the right breast, and the pillow is placed to the left side of your back and spine to examine the left breast. This keeps the breast on the front of the chest wall and tends to flatten it there. The pillow should not be overly thick. This technique allows you to feel deeply into the breast tissue even with a prosthesis beneath the breast tissue. With a prosthesis above the breast tissue self examination is not as accurate. When the breast tissue is thick or dependent (as it is when you stand or sit to examine) you can miss significant changes that are deep in the breast tissue.

Now for the right breast. Pillow in place, you will raise the right arm over your head to put the breast on a stretch, and with the fingers of your left hand extended, you feel deeply into the right breast in a rotary motion covering all quadrants of the breast, moving from the periphery to the center of the breast, the nipple area. You feel the areola and nipple region completely as well. Once you have covered all the breast in this way, then you draw the extended left hand fingers across the breast, covering it once again, in a stroking manner. This gives you two ways to evaluate the breast tissue: a) with deep point pressure and b) with a drawing or pulling of the fingers over the breast to detect any enlargements you may not have felt with the rotary pressure. Now, if anything seems different or unusual, you repeat the above maneuvers to clarify or to confirm.

Changing the pillow placement, you raise the left arm above your head and with your right hand, examine the left breast the very same way.

I stress that you lie down to examine, for when sitting in front of a mirror or standing in the shower as many women are taught to examine, your breast is compacted and dense. The breast tissue is dependent and firm, not allowing as full evaluation of it as you can if it is a thinner organ with the chest wall firmly behind it. You can miss a tissue growth when it is small and in early stages, when you do not lie down to examine.

In time, you will become very aware of any changes taking place in your breasts. Any change in the normal architecture becomes evident earlier with repetition and careful observation. Take the time to be thorough and be mindful of the need to always examine your breasts.

DEFINITIONS

Androgenic -- Any substance that mimics or is similar in activity to testosterone.

Anovulatory -- Literally means without ovulation. i.e. ovulation (egg production.)

Anti-androgen -- A substance or drug that blocks production or activity of testosterone or a testosterone like substance. Also known as an antagonist or suppressant.

Arteriosclerosis -- A thickening of the wall of an artery with cholesterol, fat, blood cells and other constituents. Also known as hardening of the arteries.

Cardiac Sparing or Protective -- Any device or medication that eases or facilitates heart activity. In the case of estrogen, this hormone lessens the arteriosclerosis process in the arteries as they supply oxygen and nutrition to the heart muscle.

Cyclic -- Recurrent activity in a particular time period i.e. progesterone production from the ovary is in the latter half of the menstrual cycle every month.

Diuretic -- A medication taken to help the body lose water that is excessive in the tissues. Water loss facilitated by such a medication takes place in the kidneys.

Electrolyte -- A chemical element necessary in our body for various reactions and processes. Sodium and potassium are very important ones.

Embolism -- When blood clots that form in blood vessels, both veins and arteries, break loose they are carried in the blood stream to different organs where they will cause damage. Example: Clots from the left side of the heart via an artery to the brain or clots from a major vein in a leg to the right side of the heart and then to the lungs.

Enzyme -- A chemical substance made in the body with a specific task or purpose. Some enzymes play definite roles in digestion. Others in cardiac or liver activity.

Gonadotropin -- A hormone that is produced in the pituitary gland and is specific in stimulating a particular organ - an endocrine gland - to perform specific functions.

Heart Attack -- This is a general term for a serious interference with normal heart function. It has come to mean a change in arterial (coronary) blood flow to the heart muscle through blockade of the blood either partial or complete. It could mean, however, change in cardiac rhythm (an arrhythmia) or problem with a damaged valve or even an attack of congestive heart failure. It is often called a cardiac accident as well.

Hyperplasia -- A swelling and increase in the cells that make up any tissue. The cells are larger and more numerous leading to increase size of the organ.

Injection -- Placement of a substance usually a drug, but it could be fluids in a muscle or other organ through a blood vessel either a vein or artery. Various terms that are associated are intramuscular (Im), subcutaneous (sub Q-- beneath the skin), or intravenous (Iv).

Phlebitis -- Inflammation in a vein, often associated with clot formation. It can often be considered an infection within the vein.

Regimen -- A protocol, a plan of therapy, a set of steps for medical treatment.

Serum -- The fluid that blood is composed of without the blood cells. Some substances are identified and measured in the laboratory in the serum only. Other substances are measured in the blood, serum and blood cells included. The terms serum and blood are often used interchangeably.

Sexual Adequacy -- The quality of sexual performance. This includes sexual appetite or libido, the erection and ejaculate and ability to experience orgasm or to bring orgasm and satisfaction to another.

Testosterone Pool -- The total amount of testosterone in the blood stream at any given time from all sources of production, both testes and both adrenal glands.

CONCLUSION

Medical care is costly—too costly at times, I believe. However, I would caution against too much cost cutting or bargain hunting in purchasing medication. Generic medication has some place in your regimen and is acceptable at some times. Keep in mind that generic medication is not as fine tuned in duration of activity and for therapeutic response as are brand name medications. Hence, while generic estrogen and progesterone could be used, they are not quite the medicines that the name brand products are.

In conclusion, overall careful evaluation on a periodic basis of one's health and the effects of hormonal therapy by a capable, knowledgeable and interested physician, should insure a comfortable life, with good health and safe progress in feminization.

It must be a cooperative effort, however. Each individual is in all reality "meddling" with their own genetic, biochemical and physical makeup. The individual should always follow directions and keep in contact with the physician as requested or required.

I hope the information given to you has been of help and that it can be an aid in making your approach to this therapy a lot less mysterious and a great deal more satisfying.